SOUL OF BERLIN

A GUIDE TO THE 30 BEST EXPERIENCES

WRITTEN BY THOMAS JONGLEZ
ILLUSTRATED BY SIRAI BUCARELLI

JONGLEZ PUBLISHING

Travel guides

"THE GREATEST CULTURAL EXTRAVAGANZA THAT ONE COULD IMAGINE."

DAVID BOWIE

This guide is for those who want to unlock the hidden doors of Berlin, feel its heartbeat, discover every last nook and cranny to uncover its soul. It's the result of three years of exploring: on foot, by bike, by metro, in the city's museums, clubs, bars, restaurants and kebab shops.

The COVID-19 pandemic obviously didn't make this task any easier. But Germany, unlike other neighbouring countries, was kind enough never to prohibit its inhabitants from leaving their homes. So when the restaurants were closed, we headed out by bike to check out the lesser-known corners of the countryside or on foot to discover neighbourhoods off the beaten track …

These explorations were an absolute delight, involving unexpected discoveries and encounters – in keeping with Berlin's extraordinary eclecticism. My top picks emerged over the course of these three years. A subjective selection, in other words, but one based on lived experiences. Of which there were definitely quite a few …

Visitors sometimes confide in me that they don't understand what's so appealing about Berlin: a harsh climate, locals who aren't always exactly welcoming, architecture that's sometimes off-putting … I usually tell them that it's because they don't live there. Indeed, if you don't know where to go when you first arrive in Berlin and simply head out on foot in search of adventure, even in the central districts, you'll quickly find yourself in a depressing no-man's-land.

This guide is for people like these, so that they'll know where to go and where not to go in order to make the most of their few days in this fabulous city. They'll discover, for example, that Berlin has beautiful beaches (yes!) and gorgeous, little-known nature spots.

But this guide is also and above all for those who live in Berlin: to help them discover or rediscover this city, so unique in the world.

Thank you, Berlin!

Thomas Jonglez

After spending a few months in the German capital in 1994 and being blown away by 'alternative' Berlin after the fall of the Wall, Thomas Jonglez took a few detours: seven months of back-packing in Latin America, seven months of driving from Beijing to Paris without ever taking a plane, six months with his family between Venice and Rio de Janeiro and across Siberia and the Pacific, three years in Brussels, three years in Paris, seven years in Venice and seven years in Rio de Janeiro ...

Returning to the loves of his youth, Thomas moved back to Berlin in 2019. What he found is a city that's obviously less alternative than it was in the 1990s but still has a particular charm and energy, to which he has paid tribute by publishing, among many other books, the *Secret Berlin* guide.

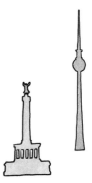

WHAT YOU WON'T FIND
IN THIS GUIDE

- a map of the Berlin underground
- the most boring starred restaurants
- how to buy your ticket for the opera
- practical information on getting to the top of the Fernsehturm

WHAT YOU WILL FIND
IN THIS GUIDE

- the world's smallest nightclub
- Berlin's best beaches
- the most beautiful bike ride
- a fabulous spa that'll make you feel like you're in Bali
- an ice cream shop that makes its own cones right in front of you
- where to go kayaking, just like in Venice
- the best places to have lunch by the water
- how to spend a night in a mattress workshop

SYMBOLS USED IN
"SOUL OF BERLIN"

Less
than €30

€30
to €90

More
than €90

So
Berlin

Opening times often vary,
so we recommend checking them directly
on the website of the place you plan to visit.

30 EXPERIENCES

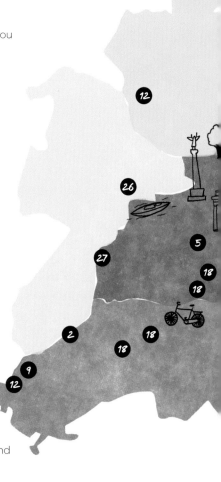

THE ICE CREAM SHOP
THAT MAKES
ITS OWN CONES

Famous in the neighbourhood (the queues can be long in the warm months), Jones is one of Berlin's most famous ice-cream makers – the best, even, according to some fans. But what really makes it unique is that they make their own cones, right in front of their customers. You can also get a traditional cone for a bit less, but why would you skip the house speciality?

And (the cherry on the top, as it were): Jones also has excellent cookies – homemade, naturally.

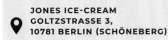

JONES ICE-CREAM
GOLTZSTRASSE 3,
10781 BERLIN (SCHÖNEBERG)

| DAILY: noon / 7 pm | 041 523 0034 | U7 (Eisenacher Straße) |

HAPPY
TRAILS

The south-west of Berlin is a true natural paradise: the gorgeous bike ride along the Wannsee (see p. 44) can also be done on foot, and the shores of the Schlachtensee, Krumme Lanke and Grunewaldsee also present opportunities for a wonderful day out – or more, depending on your pace.

In the north, you can walk around the Grunewaldsee in about 1 to 1½ hours. Just make sure to stop for a drink on the beautiful terrace of Jagdschloss Grunewald, a hunting lodge with a remarkably peaceful atmosphere. (You can also visit the interesting museum inside, consisting mainly of paintings by Lucas Cranach the Elder.) Lunch in a beer-garden atmosphere is an option just a few steps away at 12 Apostoli am Grunewaldsee. And, needless to say, going for a swim in the lake is de rigueur in summer.

 **WALKS AROUND THE SCHLACHTENSEE,
KRUMME LANKE
AND GRUNEWALDSEE LAKES**

Getting there: Schlachtensee and Krumme Lanke: S1, S2 (Schlachtensee) and U3 (Krumme Lanke) Grunewaldsee: U3 (Oskar-Helene-Heim), then a (pleasant) 25-minute walk or the X10 Bus followed by a 15-minute walk

Further south, after circling Krumme Lanke lake (approx. 1 hour), you'll reach the delightful Schlachtensee, which has a particularly pleasant holiday atmosphere (and takes about 2 to 2½ hours to walk around). Descending one of the flights of stairs

leading down to its southern shore is a spectacular experience. Skip the restaurant at the north-eastern corner of the lake – you're better off bringing a picnic and finding your own little corner of paradise, from where you can also enjoy a fantastic swim.

INDUSTRIAL
CULTURE

Built between 1960 and 1964, the former urban power station known as Kraftwerk encapsulates a whole piece of Berlin's industrial and party history. Home to the famous techno club Tresor since 2006, today it's also a spectacular setting for exhibitions, concerts and dance performances.

The space isn't open every day, so make sure to check the programme on the website and book your tickets in advance.

KRAFTWERK
KÖPENICKER STR. 70,
10179 BERLIN (KREUZBERG)

| Reservations
highly recommended | kraftwerkberlin.de | U8 (Heinrich Heine) |

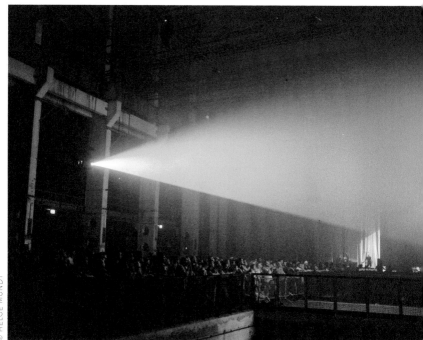

PLAYING PING PONG
IN BERLIN

Don't forget your ping pong racket when you come to Berlin, my tourist friend. Real Berliners know that the city's a paradise for table tennis players. There are hundreds – yes, hundreds! – of ping pong tables scattered around town, available for anyone to use, just waiting for you.

Where? We're eternally grateful to the brilliant Peter Ulrich for creating the amazing 'Ping Pong Map' app, which clearly pinpoints all the city's tables. But beware: some are in schools and therefore off limits.

pingpongmap.net/Berlin

THE TASTE OF
OLD BERLIN

Few cities in the world have as many authentic historic restaurants as Berlin. Despite the war, despite the Wall, despite the Nazis, several charming hang-outs where you can while away the hours have managed to survive. Places you go to not necessarily for the quality of the food but to soak up the timeless atmosphere, undisturbed.

> **Josep-Roth-Diele**

One of our favourite spots, named after the Austrian Jewish writer Joseph Roth (1894–1939), who lived next door until 1933, when he was forced into exile. Except for the ceiling, the room is authentically vintage (1898), with a delightful atmosphere and retro music. Very good crème caramel … and the day's newspapers are on offer too.

JOSEPH-ROTH-DIELE
POTSDAMER STR. 75,
10785 BERLIN (TIERGARTEN)

| MON–FRI: 10am / 10pm | 030 26369884
info@joseph-roth-diele.de
joseph-roth-diele.de | U1, U3 (Kurfürstenstraße) |

© BERTRAND SAINT GUILHEM

> E. & M. Leydicke

Opened by Emil and Max Leydicke in 1877, Leydicke is a little jewel far from the trends and the crowds – the decor doesn't seem to have changed since the place opened. The colourful owner, Raimon Marquardt, still distils homemade liqueurs, which he serves on the premises or to take away.

We love to linger here, savouring the unique atmosphere. A rare spot.

E. & M. LEYDICKE
MANSTEINSTRAßE 4,
10783 BERLIN (SCHÖNEBERG)

| DAILY: 6pm / 11pm | 030 2162973
leydicke.com | U7 (Yorckstraße) |

> Alt Berliner Wirtshaus Henne ▲

A delightful spot. Opened in 1908 (in a building dating from 1888), 'Henne' survived for a long time just 5 metres from the Berlin Wall.

Today, you can enjoy a wonderful fried half-chicken (secret recipe) with traditional potato salad or coleslaw.

Not to be missed!

ALT-BERLINER WIRTSHAUS HENNE
LEUSCHNERDAMM 25,
10999 BERLIN (KREUZBERG)

| TUE–SUN: 5pm / 10pm | Reservations highly recommended
030 6147730
henne-berlin.de | U1, U3 (Kottbusser Tor) |

> Diener Tattersall

Opened in 1893, the superb Diener Tattersall, always packed to the rafters, is a place where you're likely to experience intense encounters. Taken over by former boxer Franz Diener in the 1950s, it has become a must for artists and Berlin's beautiful people (note the 500 or so portraits of artists that adorn the walls), who love to hang out in the relaxed atmosphere there. A real institution.

DIENER TATTERSALL
GROLMANSTRASSE 47,
10623 BERLIN (CHARLOTTENBURG)

| MON–SAT: 6pm / 2am | Reservations highly recommended 030 8815329 diener-berlin.de | U7 (Yorckstraße) |

A SPA EXPERIENCE THAT WILL TRANSPORT YOU
TO BALI

To survive the long Berlin winter, you have two options: fly to the tropics or head to the fantastic Vabali Spa.

Covering no less than 20,000 m², Vabali, with its four outdoor baths, two pools, seven saunas and four hammams, is a little gem where you'll always end up spending more time than you expected. The Balinese-style decoration feels very authentic, the massages are high quality (book in advance), there's a Southeast-Asian-inspired restaurant, plenty of beds (including some waterbeds) and seating options for resting, fireplaces ... This is a little oasis of peace that's not to be missed. For the ultimate relaxation, enjoy the winter sun in the small outdoor baths around the main pool: pure bliss.

Some practical advice: the outdoor floors are cold in winter, so bring your own flip-flops (and a bathrobe and towel, for that matter) so you don't have to rent them. There's no need to bring swimwear, however: nudity is compulsory in the pools, saunas and hammams, though you can of course keep your bathrobe on the rest of the time (and your towel in the saunas).

 VABALI SPA
SEYDLITZSTRASSE 6,
10557 BERLIN (MOABIT)

| DAILY: 9am / midnight | Reservations highly recommended | U1, U5, S3, S5, S7, S9 (Hauptbahnhof), then a 15-minute walk |

A MASTERPIECE OF
SILENT CINEMA WITH A LIVE ORCHESTRA

About twice a month, the legendary Babylon Mitte offers the chance to see Fritz Lang's 1927 masterpiece of silent cinema, the mythical *Metropolis*, in exceptional conditions. At the heart of the enormous auditorium with its art deco vibe, an orchestra some thirty musicians strong provides a musical accompaniment for two and a half hours, evoking the glory days of pre-war cinema, when every screening was a true performance.

Remember to book in advance on the cinema's website so you're sure to get a seat.

The Babylon also lets you (re)discover other cool silent films accompanied by an organ every Saturday night at midnight – free of charge. 0:00 am, 0€, 0 dialogue – a programme as original as it is minimalist.

METROPOLIS AT THE BABYLON
ROSA-LUXEMBURG-STRASSE 30, 10178
BERLIN (MITTE)

| Reservations highly recommended | babylonberlin.eu | U2 (Rosa-Luxemburg-Platz) |

A ONE-OF-A-KIND CINEMA

Opened in 1963, a few minutes' walk from Alexanderplatz, it retains its inimitable East German atmosphere despite renovations after the fall of the Wall – especially in the upstairs bar, where you can have a drink under chandeliers from the former Czechoslovakia. Then there's the 17.5-metre screen, a large auditorium that seats 608 (currently 551) and impeccable acoustics, thanks in particular to the wave-shaped ceiling ... If the Funkhaus (see p. 65) wasn't enough to convince you that they also knew how to build quality buildings in East Germany, head on over to Kino International.

KINO INTERNATIONAL KARL-MARX-ALLEE 33, 10178 BERLIN (MITTE)

yorck.de/kinos/kino-international
U-Bahn (Schillingstraße)

THE MAGIC OF OPEN-AIR CINEMA

One of the great pleasures of summer in Berlin is catching a film under the open skies. The city is teeming with great open-air cinemas in every district, whether in parks (Hasenheide, Rehberge) or in gardens right in the heart of the city. Our favourites are the ones in Kreuzberg (behind the Künstlerhaus Bethanien) and especially the Pompeji in Ostkreuz (in the grounds of the ZUKUNFT cultural centre).

FREILUFTKINO (OPEN-AIR CINEMA)
Various locations: openair-kino.net

OSTKREUZ
zukunft-ostkreuz.de/freiluftkino.html
(NB: this brilliant spot – with indoor & outdoor cinemas, a bar, a concert hall, etc. – is under threat of closure, so hurry on over there right now!)

KREUZBERG
freiluftkino-kreuzberg.de
From May to approx. mid-September

THE BEST BURGERS
IN TOWN

While there's nothing but good food at Markt Halle Neun (market hall 9), the burgers at Kumpel & Keule definitely stand out: they are, quite simply, the best in Berlin – by far. The quality of the meat is unparalleled, they're cooked to perfection, and the ingredients and sauce are memorable ...

Kumpel & Keule is also a butcher's shop that sells excellent (obviously!) meat.

After enjoying an outstanding burger, take a walk around and finish off your lunch with a crêpe, tiramisu or coffee at one of the stalls in this covered market, which dates back to 1891 – one of the last (and most well-preserved) of the 14 covered markets that opened in Berlin at the end of the 19th century.

While you're here, don't forget to shop for cheese, vegetables, fruit and fish – expensive but delicious.

 KUMPEL & KEULE GMBH
MARKTHALLE NEUN
EISENBAHNSTRASSE 42–43,
10997 BERLIN (KREUZBERG)

MON–SAT: 9am / 6pm Usually open on Thursday evening	kumpelundkeule.de markthalleneun.de	U1, U3 (Görlitzer Bahnhof)

BERLIN'S MOST BEAUTIFUL **CYCLING ROUTE**

It's no secret to Berliners, but not many tourists know that the German capital is a little paradise for nature lovers and cyclists. South-west of Berlin (but still within the official city limits), you can spend an amazing day between the Wannsee S-Bahn station and northern Potsdam.

Some tips:

- Ideally, choose a nice, warm sunny day so you can go for a swim every now and then. Leave early because the route is so pleasant and wide-ranging that it can take all day if you want.

- Take your bike on the S-Bahn to Wannsee (or rent a bike when you get there). Exit on the west side (towards the water), cross the bridge (Wannseebrücke) and take the first right onto Am Großen Wannsee. There are two places where you might stop along the way, both on the right: the Max Liebermann Museum, with its charming garden overlooking the lake, and the Haus der Wannsee Konferenz (infamous for its role in the Holocaust), which has an interesting historical exhibition and a lovely garden overlooking the water. Once you reach the end of this street, the rest of the route takes you along an exceptionally pleasant, car-free path.

- About halfway along the route (20 to 30 minutes by bike), we recommend taking the ferry to visit Pfaueninsel (Peacock Island) on foot. You can enjoy a well-earned drink sitting on a deckchair overlooking the water, next to the pier – a better location than the restaurant behind it.

- Back on the mainland, pedal on for another 15 to 20 minutes to discover a corner of paradise: the small natural cove of Moorlake with the Wirtshaus Moorlake (Moorlake Inn), where you can stop for a delicious lunch. There are a number of beaches along the

way, some larger than others, where you can take a welcome dip. The one in front of the restaurant, though small, is an absolute must. Cycling on, you'll catch sight of the charming Italianate Heilandskirche (Church of the Redeemer) on the other side of the Wannsee.

- Continue along the waterfront path to the beautiful Glienicke Park, where you can visit the small museum in the palace, stroll through the gardens and enjoy a meal in the beautiful inner courtyard. The route concludes with a ride across the Glienicke Brücke (the famous bridge where spies were exchanged during the GDR era) and then, keeping to the right, to the sublime Kongsnaes Restaurant, where you can round off the day with dinner (reservations recommended, see p. 62). The view from the terrace is exceptional.

- To get back to Berlin, turn back along the water or, if it's already dark, take the S-Bahn from Babelsberg in Potsdam (a shorter and nicer route than the direct one to the Wannsee S-Bahn station).

HERE ARE SOME OTHER LOVELY CYCLING ROUTES IN THE HEART OF NATURE:

- From Schlachtensee to Grunewaldsee via Krumme Lanke, going round all three lakes; you can also do this route on foot (south-west of Berlin – Nikolassee S-Bahn station) – see p. 17.
- Along the north-west shore of Tegeler See (north-west Berlin – Alt Tegel station on the U6).
- Along Treptower Park and Plänterwald (Treptow – Treptower Park S-Bahn station).
- From Wendenschloss beach (see p. 85), along the water's edge, to Große Krampe. You can continue on from there along the waterside to Seddinsee, but the path is pretty rough (Köpenick – Grünau S-Bahn station).
- Along Meskengraben, starting from the U7 Rudow station: a truly rural atmosphere.
- In Lübars, north of Berlin, starting from Hermsdorfer See, passing near the Lübars beach (where we recommend making a stop: see p. 84), to the village of Alt-Lübars, where you can have lunch or dinner across from the church on the terrace of the Alter Dorfkrug Inn (recommended for its location more than anything else) (S-Bahn: Waidmannslust station, then Bus 222).

AN EXCEPTIONAL
AESTHETIC EXPERIENCE

Located in Kreuzberg, in a former Second World War bunker converted by the architect John Pawson, the Feuerle Collection is an exceptional private collection of ancient Khmer and Chinese art open for viewing by appointment only.

The visit, which lasts a total of one hour, is a true aesthetic, spiritual and erotic experience, the collection of ancient art being interspersed with works of art by Cristina Iglesias, Anish Kapoor and others, as well as contemporary photographs.

More well-to-do patrons can rent the venue to visit it at their leisure but also and above all to enjoy a unique olfactory experience in private: an Incense Ceremony that lasts about 45 minutes.

The collection is named after Désiré Feuerle, the founder (together with Sara Puig) of this exhibition space, which promises visitors the feeling of a moment outside of time.

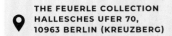

THE FEUERLE COLLECTION
HALLESCHES UFER 70,
10963 BERLIN (KREUZBERG)

| Reservations required | thefeuerlecollection.org/en | U1, U3, U7 (Möckernbrücke) |

THE WORLD'S
SMALLEST
NIGHTCLUB

Didn't get into Berghain? Or Katerblau? Then head on over to Teledisko!

There's no chance of being turned away at the door here: just slide 2€ into the slot, choose your tunes and enter this phone-booth-sized nightclub with whoever you want: your dog, two or five friends ...

Three minutes of pure magic – and there's even a disco ball.

TELEDISKO
RAW-GELÄNDE
REVALER STR. 99,
10245 BERLIN (FRIEDRICHSHAIN)

teledisko.com

U1, U3, S3, S5, S7, S9 (Warschauer Straße)

LUNCH AL FRESCO
AT THE WATER'S EDGE

Few capitals in Europe – in the world, even – have terraces where you can have lunch by the water in the middle of the city. Here is an overview of the best places to make you feel like you're on holiday the moment the weather gets nice.

> A small corner of paradise

Wirtshaus Moorlake is nestled in a veritable paradise along the Wannsee, southwest of Berlin (see p. 44). It's an exceptionally peaceful and tranquil setting for a perfect lunch – and an excuse to enjoy a wonderful day in the countryside, topped off by a marvellous swim.

MOORLAKE
MOORLAKEWEG 6,
14109 BERLIN (WANNSEE)

Lunch only   030 8055809   moorlake.de

> **The terrace at the end of the world**

The best spot at the water's edge northwest of Berlin. Slightly hidden away and thus not very well known, Fahrhaus Saatwinkel serves magnificent salmon, smoked on site by the owner. After lunch on the spacious and beautiful terrace, you can take the ferry to the idyllic little island of Maienwerder to go for a stroll. If you add on biking to the ferry and going for the compulsory dip (while waiting for the ferry, for example), you're sure to enjoy a wonderful day that will make you feel like you're far away from everything.

 FAHRHAUS SAATWINKEL
IM SAATWINKEL 15,
13599 BERLIN (SPANDAU)

faehrhaus-saatwinkel.de

> **A floating restaurant near Müggelsee** ▲

Taking the mini ferry to SpreeArche, a floating restaurant in eastern Köpenick (east of Berlin), is a small delight. (It's also a great opportunity to spend the day in the countryside, tooling around on a bike.) The smoked salmon is excellent – and the welcome particularly friendly.

 SPREEARCHE
MÜGGELSCHLÖSSCHENWEG 0,
12559 BERLIN (KÖPENICK)

Open in winter when the weather's good; lunch at weekends only Open daily in fine weather – but it's best to call ahead to make a reservation.	0172- 304 21 11	info@spreearche.de

> An exceptional view

At the entrance to Potsdam, after the Glienicke Bridge just outside of Berlin, a superb view awaits you on the terrace of the restaurant Kongsnaes. Reservations are recommended.

KONGSNAES
SCHWANENALLEE 7D,
14467 POTSDAM

| FRI–SUN: lunch and dinner | Reservations highly recommended | kongsnaes.de |

> **A terrace in the heart of the city** ▲

Along the Kreuzberg canal, a few steps from the Spree, Freischwimmer has a beautiful terrace for enjoying lunch or a drink in the sun.

 FREISCHWIMMER
VOR DEM SCHLESISCHEN TOR 2,
10997 BERLIN (KREUZBERG)

freischwimmer-berlin.com

EAST GERMANY
AT THE TOP
OF ITS GAME

The Funkhaus is an amazing place. Headquarters of the East German state radio until 1990, the building – designed by Franz Ehrlich in 1951 – is a masterpiece of 1950s architecture.

Today, the vast 13-hectare complex offers exciting guided tours (the fantastic staircase that leads nowhere, designed with different surfaces to make it possible to record the nuances of footsteps on the stairs, is particularly impressive), concerts (some of which take place in the world's largest music recording studio) and sound performances.

After lunch in one of the Funkhaus's two restaurants, you could spend a delightful afternoon and evening on the terrace next to the Spree, which you can also explore by renting a kayak a few metres away.

© UWE FABICH

 FUNKHAUS
NALEPASTRASSE 18,
12459 BERLIN (RUMMELSBURG)

| 030 12085416 | info@funkhaus-berlin.net
tickets@funkhaus-berlin.net
funkhaus-berlin.net | Tram 21 (Blockdammweg) |

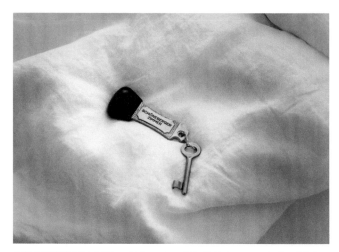

SPEND A NIGHT IN
A UNIQUE MATTRESS WORKSHOP

Working out of a beautiful flat in a classic building in Schöneberg, Daniel Heer is one of the last four manufacturers of exceptional mattresses in Europe: made exclusively by hand, using traditional techniques, his horsehair mattresses are guaranteed for life.

To allow his customers to test the quality of his mattresses under the best conditions, this passionate artisan had the wonderful idea of letting them spend one night – and one night only – in a room in his workshop.

After you've enjoyed a long and exceptionally restful sleep, Daniel will serve you breakfast (in the courtyard garden, weather permitting), giving you the perfect chance to discuss his know-how or the best places in the neighbourhood.

DANIEL HEER
SCHÖNEBERGER ZIMMER
BLUMENTHALSTRASSE 7,
10783 BERLIN (TIERGARTEN)

030 81475123
danielheer.com

U1, U3 (Kurfürstenstrasse)

For dinner, you can head to the charming Oh, Panama Restaurant, just a stone's throw from the workshop. The nearby Victoria Bar (great for cocktails!) is also a sure bet, as is the Kumpelnest 3000 Bar/nightclub, with its slightly more

eccentric vibe. For experimental music, the tiny Au Topsy Pohl Bar is also close by, as is the more traditional but no less pleasant Joseph-Roth-Diele Restaurant (see p. 26).

(see p. 26).

THE BEST RESTAURANTS
IN NEUKÖLLN

Neukölln is the district of Berlin with the city's coolest bars and restaurants. Here are our top picks.

> **Our kind of restaurant**

Located in the very pleasant Schillerkiez, not far from Tempelhof, Barra is our kind of restaurant: lovely decor, top-quality cuisine, friendly service, reasonable prices ... In fact, you'll eat better here than in many starred restaurants and you'll always have a better time. So definitely not to be missed – make sure to book several days in advance.

 BARRA
OKERSTRASSE 2,
12049 BERLIN (NEUKÖLLN)

MON–FRI: 6:30pm / 10:30pm	Reservations highly recommended 030 818 60757 reservations@barraberlin.com	U8 (Leinestraße)

> Exceptional ice cream at an excellent pizzeria

Gazzo Pizzeria is one of Berlin's best pizzerias: dough that's crispy (just a touch, exactly the way we like it), quality ingredients, original combinations of toppings. But Gazzo has a secret weapon: its exceptional ice cream, made with buffalo milk from Brandenburg and eaten with a drizzle of olive oil (yes, really!), which makes all the difference.

 GAZZO PIZZERIA
HOBRECHTSTRASSE 57,
12047 BERLIN (NEUKÖLLN)

DAILY: noon / 10pm | gazzopizza.com | U8 (Schönleinstraße)

© SORREL

> The perfect brunch

One of our favourite places in Berlin. Modern but cosy decor, simple but good food (don't skip the fantastic croque monsieur or the French toast with crème fraîche), very cool welcome ... What's not to love? Another advantage: Sorrel is one of the few good restaurants in Berlin that's open for lunch.

SORREL
PANNIERSTRASSE 40,
12047 BERLIN (NEUKÖLLN)

| SAT–MON and WED: 10am / 5pm THU & FRI: 10am / 11pm | Reservations highly recommended 030 84711195 | U1, U3 (Görlitzer Bahnhof) or U7, U8 (Hermannplatz) then about a 10-minute walk |

#16

IMMERSE YOURSELF IN THE BERLIN OF
THE ROARING TWENTIES

Located in north-east Berlin, largely off the beaten tourist track, the Delphi is a magnificent cinema built in 1929. Abandoned for a long time, it was revived as a performance venue in 2017.

Head there to experience the still-perceptible atmosphere of 1920s Berlin and the Weimar Republic: several scenes for the TV series *Babylon Berlin* were filmed here, even though plenty of Berliners don't even know the place exists.

You can have a drink at the friendly Brotfabrik next door before or after the show. And while you're in the somewhat outlying district of Weißensee, try to spend the day in the area by visiting the exceptional Jewish cemetery (see p. 104) and charming Orankesee beach (see p. 84).

 **THEATER IM DELPHI**
GUSTAV-ADOLF-STRASSE 2,
13086 BERLIN (WEISSENSEE)

| Reservations highly recommended | theater-im-delphi.de | U2, S2, S8, S41, S42, S85 (Schönhauser Allee) |

BERLIN'S
BEST BEACHES

Berliners may know about them (though often they're only familiar with the one at Wannsee and, at best, two or three others), but visitors are always amazed: yes, when the weather's nice in Berlin, there are real sandy beaches if you feel like a swim – right in the city.

There are eleven official *Strandbäder*: beaches with an affordable admission fee and a small kiosk serving drinks and snacks – and sometimes even a modest restaurant. Open from around mid-May to mid-September, they also provide sunbeds (often for an extra fee) and the mythical *Strandkörbe* ('beach baskets'), a charming throwback to the pre-war years. No more getting a crick in your neck lying on your towel on the city's small free beaches; instead, stretch out comfortably on your sun lounger and immerse yourself in a book or calmly take in the surroundings, including the beach volleyball and ping-pong players. (Courts and tables are provided: to join in the fun, just bring your own equipment.) It's almost like being in Rio.

Of these official beaches, our favourites are:

> **Strandbad Orankesee**

One of the lesser-known beaches, Orankesee offers everything the classic beaches do but in an especially lovely atmosphere and setting. Plus, it's the closest to the city centre: about 10 to 15 minutes by car from Mitte, 10 minutes from Prenzlauer Berg and 15 to 20 minutes from Kreuzberg.
Gertrudstraße 7 – 13053 Berlin (Weißensee)
strandbad-orankesee.de

> **Strandbad Lübars** ▼

A nice surprise in the north of Berlin. Very pleasant and spacious, with a proper restaurant overlooking the lake.
Am Freibad 9 – 13469 Berlin (Reinickensdorf)
berlinerbaeder.de

> Strandbad Plötzensee

A beautiful setting, with a younger, more festive atmosphere at the end of the day. You can also go for lovely walks in the nearby forest.

Nordufer 26 – 13351 Berlin (Wedding)
berlinerbaeder.de

> Strandbad Wendenschloss

Wide expanses of sand and grass and a proper restaurant. Easy to reach by bike from the Grünau S-Bahn station and then by ferry across Langer See. And you can continue on from there, taking a beautiful bike ride to the south-east, down along Langer See.

Möllhausenufer 30 – 12557 Berlin (Köpenick)
strandbad-wendenschloss.berlin

WHERE CAN YOU GO SKINNY DIPPING IN BERLIN?

The city has several nudist beaches (known as FKK for *Freikörperkultur* – 'free body culture'), officially located at Flughafensee Tegel, Strandbad Plötzensee, Teufelsee (Grunewald), Halensee, Grunewaldsee, Krumme Lanke and Strandbad Müggelsee (which isn't a real private beach like the others).
For those who like to swim in the buff (understandable) but prefer to avoid the crowds, there are also many discreet places along Berlin's lakes and rivers where you can strip naked, either to go for a swim or just to dry off. Discretion is recommended but Berliners tend to be quite tolerant when it comes to nudity.

EXPLORE
LITTLE-KNOWN
ARCHITECTURAL
MASTERPIECES

Despite the destruction caused by the Second World War, several architectural gems – most of them unfamiliar even to locals – managed to survive in Berlin, as did some unique architectural curiosities. There are also some amazing post-war buildings. What follows is a short, though hardly exhaustive, list.

> A masterpiece of brutalist architecture

With a shape reminiscent of a giant warship, the Mäusebunker (literally, 'mouse bunker') is one of Berlin's most spectacular and little-known buildings. A 120-metre-long masterpiece of brutalist architecture, this exceptional building was designed by the Berlin architect Gerd Hänska, together with his wife and son, as an animal experimentation laboratory for the Freie Universität between 1967 and 1970. Today, the building is no longer in use and is not open to the public.

> **MÄUSEBUNKER**
> **KRAHMERSTRASSE 6,**
> **12207 BERLIN (ZEHLENDORF)**

Only the exterior of the building can be viewed | S25, S26 (Lichterfelde Ost)

> An expressionist wonder

Built between 1927 and 1929 and based on the plans of Ernst Paulus and his son Günther Paulus, the Kreuzkirche (Church of the Cross) is a masterpiece of expressionist architecture.

Stop and admire its surprising blue-glazed ceramic entrance portal and, above all, its remarkable octagonal main hall – the wonderful painted wall decorations behind the altar are also typically expressionistic.

The entrance door to the parish offices, about 10 metres to the left of the church's main entrance as you walk up Hohenzollerndamm towards the S-Bahn, also has some fantastic expressionist ornamentation.

 KREUZKIRCHE
HOHENZOLLERNDAMM 130A,
14199 BERLIN (SCHMARGENDORF)

SAT: 4pm / 6pm (also SUN for Mass at 11am)	030 83224663 kreuzkirche-berlin.de	S41 (Hohenzollerndamm)

> A masterpiece of light

Built between 1930 and 1933 and based on the designs of Ossip Klarwein, the church at Hohenzollernplatz is one of the most interesting examples of expressionist architecture in Berlin. The lateral windows and huge stained glass window behind the altar produce remarkable light effects, with the pale cement arches reflecting shades of yellow, red and blue, intensifying the mystical atmosphere of the place.

 CHURCH AT HOHENZOLLERNPLATZ
NASSAUISCHE STRASSE 66–67,
10717 BERLIN (WILMERSDORF)

TUE & THU: 2pm / 6pm
WED & FRI: 11am / 1pm
SAT: 1pm / 3pm and also open for events and Masses
(sung Mass every Saturday at noon)

U2, U3 (Hohenzollernplatz)

> Out-of-the-ordinary chimneys

In the rather drab south of Schöneberg, the large Malzfabrik building along Bessemerstraße boasts four spectacular chimneys topped with metal extensions that turn in the wind. Far from being smoke extractors, they were actually designed to capture fresh air to optimise beer production in the (former) factory below.

 CHIMNEYS OF THE MALZFABRIK
BESSEMERSTRASSE 2–14,
12103 BERLIN (SCHÖNEBERG)

Guided tours ('Malzreise') on reservation:
tunneltours.de/project/industrie
17.50€ per person (no discounts)

S41, S42, S45, S46 (Tempelhof)
S2, S25, S26 (Südkreuz)

> Futuristic pop-art architecture

Built in 1976 by the architects Ralf Schüler and his wife Ursulina Schüler-Witte as a restaurant (the Steglitz Tower), the Bierpinsel is a small masterpiece of futuristic pop-art architecture and one of the few surviving buildings from the 1970s. The 46-metre-tall building, once a bar, restaurant and club, is no longer in use. Its name, derived from Berlin slang, means 'beer brush': designed in the shape of a tree (or brush, in some people's eyes), it was originally simply a watering hole that served plenty of beer to its regulars.

BIERPINSEL
SCHLOSSSTRASSE 17,
12163 BERLIN (STEGLITZ)

U9 (Schloßstraße)

> One of Berlin's most beautiful interiors

Not many Berliners have stepped foot inside the Landgericht Berlin (Berlin Regional Court), built in 1904 by the architects Paul Thoemer, Rudolf Mönnich and Otto Schmalz. Yet hidden inside is one of the most beautiful interiors in the city, a mix of art nouveau, rococo and neo-Gothic styles. To enter, you have to show your passport or official identity card.

ATRIUM OF THE BERLIN REGIONAL COURT
LITTENSTRAßE, 12–17
10179 BERLIN (MITTE)

MON–FRI: 9am / 1pm

U2 (Klosterstraße)

#19

A TRUE
GOURMET
EXPERIENCE

So-called gourmet restaurants, whether in Berlin or elsewhere in the world, are often underwhelming: pretentious, boring, simply not very good ...

Ernst is the exact opposite. Sure, it's expensive, but the ingredients and cooking are so exceptional that it quickly becomes clear that the prices are fully justified.

Just take a look at the chef, Dylan Watson-Brawn, a Canadian from Vancouver who moved to Berlin after several years at the three-Michelin-star restaurant RyuGin in Tokyo: the passion that moves him and his taste for perfection, creativity and novelty guarantee an exceptional experience.

The restaurant's small size (seven seats at the counter) and the sophistication of the dishes and cutlery – everything here is designed to create an unforgettable evening.

ERNST
GERICHTSTRASSE 54,
13347 BERLIN (WEDDING)

| WED–SAT: 7:30pm / midnight
Reservations required | ernstberlin.de | U6 (Wedding) |

A NIGHT OUT IN
1990S BERLIN

A bit to the east of the city (20 minutes by taxi from Kreuzberg), in the Oberschönerweide district, MaHalla Berlin is located in a spectacular space: a former light-bulb factory that has also been used as a showroom.

Here, MaHalla holds regular parties and performances, which are always amazing: it feels like being in Berlin in the 1990s. Subscribe to their newsletter to keep informed of their events.

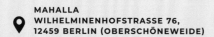

MAHALLA
WILHELMINENHOFSTRASSE 76,
12459 BERLIN (OBERSCHÖNEWEIDE)

info@mahalla.berlin
mahalla.berlin

S8, S9, S45, S46, S47, S85
(Schöneweide)

A JOURNEY
INTO THE LIGHT

Since 2015, at the heart of the historic Dorotheenstadt cemetery in Mitte, a little-known work by the famous American artist James Turrell has been on display, open to the public by reservation.

As always with Turrell, you can expect the most spectacular optical effects half an hour before sunset (which varies depending on the time of year). This is the moment when the changing light outside blends with the evolving colours projected inside the cemetery chapel – based on the same principle used by the artist on the Japanese island of Naoshima.

LIGHT INSTALLATION BY JAMES TURRELL
CHAPEL AT THE DOROTHEENSTADT CEMETERY
(DOROTHEENSTÄDTISCHER FRIEDHOF I)
CHAUSSEESTRASSE 126, 10115 BERLIN

From September to May, by reservation only	For opening hours, see the website: evfbs.de	U6 (Naturkundemuseum)

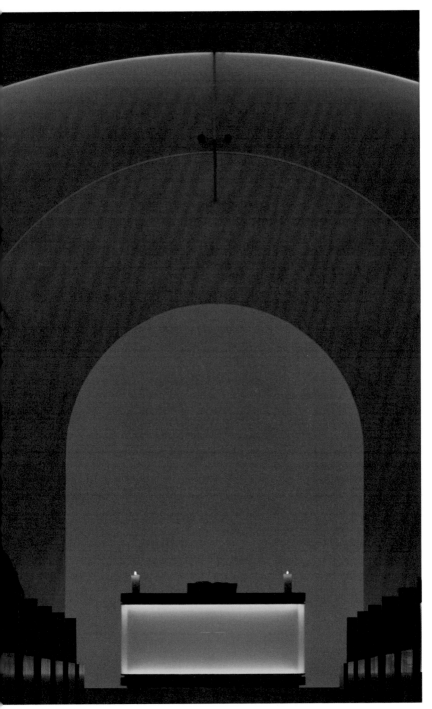

STROLLING THROUGH ONE OF THE WORLD'S **MOST BEAUTIFUL CEMETERIES**

The Jewish cemetery in Berlin-Weißensee must be one of the most beautiful in the world – and it has the great advantage of not being crowded as it's located at some distance from the city centre. It's lovely to wander along the shady paths of this cemetery with its nostalgic, romantic atmosphere. It was founded in 1880 and most of the graves date to before the First World War.

There are many magnificent graves in the middle of what seems like an enchanted urban forest. The most beautiful (which isn't well known) is a real gem: ask for a map at the entrance and look for the grave of the Lewinsohn and Netter families, which dates from 1893, at the intersection of rows IIA, IIB, IIG and IIH.

 WEIßENSEE JEWISH CEMETERY
HERBERT-BAUM-STRASSE 45,
13088 BERLIN (WEIßENSEE)

MON–THU: 7:30am / 5pm
FRI: 7:30am / 2:30pm

Tram M4 (Albertinenstraße)

And don't miss the intersection of rows IIK, IIJ, IIR and IIS: this small square contains an exceptional collection of graves, especially the art nouveau-inspired ones of the Adam, Friedlaender and Baszynski families.

While you're in the area, an ideal way to round off the day is to head to the beautiful Orankesee beach (see p. 84), take a walk around the Weißensee and Obersee lakes and end the evening with a show at the sublime Theater im Delphi (see p. 80).

THE WORLD'S
BEST TECHNO

Berlin's clubs are the best in the world – by far: they're open all year round (not like in Ibiza, for example) and, above all, 24 hours a day in some cases, from Friday night to Monday morning. What other city on the planet lets you dance to the sounds of the world's best DJs on Saturday at 4pm or on Sunday evening at dinner time (a favourite slot for many Berlin clubbers, after the tourists have left)? Almost none.

Berlin quickly adopted techno, which was born in Detroit (USA) in the 1980s, right after the fall of the Wall: the city's many wild, illegal parties became the symbol of freedom rediscovered. Today, while there are still a few illegal raves here and there, techno is played mainly in out-of-the-ordinary clubs where photo bans are the norm, so that people can let loose without having to fear any repercussions on social media.

It isn't always easy to get into some of these clubs: countless people have been turned away from the mythical Berghain,

	BERGHAIN AM WRIEZENER BHF, 10243 BERLIN (FRIEDRICHSHAIN)	SISYPHOS HAUPTSTR. 15, 10317 BERLIN (RUMMELSBURG)	HEIDEGLÜHEN (CHARLOTTENBURG NORD)
	berghain.berlin/de	sisyphos-berlin.net	No specific address; a trip to the Heideglühen has to be earned …! heidegluehen.berlin

even after queuing for hours in the cold or rain. A word of advice: try to avoid Friday and Saturday nights.

Apart from the legendary and de rigueur Berghain, another favourite of ours is Sisyphos (Rummelsburg, 10–15 minutes by car from Kreuzberg), with its fantastic DJs, garden, café, several rooms and slightly ramshackle, very 90s-Berlin atmosphere. In summer, you can dance outside in the sun. We're also fans of Club der Visionäre and the smaller but also excellent Heideglühen (which is less techno-oriented than the others), as well as Kater Blau, where, among other things, you can enjoy dancing outside and on the banks of the Spree.

CLUB DER VISIONÄRE AM FLUTGRABEN, 12435 BERLIN (KREUZBERG)	**KATER BLAU** HOLZMARKTSTRASSE 25, 10243 BERLIN (FRIEDRICHSHAIN)
clubdervisionaere.com	katerblau.de

EXPLORING
UNDERGROUND
BERLIN

Unterwelten is an association of guides specialising in forbidden underground spots with links to Nazi Germany or erstwhile East Germany: former bunkers, tunnels dug to circumvent the Wall ...

No matter which circuit you choose, these tours are an absolute must-do, thanks to the talented guides (who speak many languages) and their first-rate explanations, not to mention the places themselves.

At the association's headquarters in Gesundbrunnen, in north Berlin (don't linger in the area, which isn't the city's most attractive), there's a fascinating exhibition on 'Germania', the outrageous Nazi project for a Reich capital that was never built.

Whatever you do, don't miss out on these tours.

UNTERWELTEN
BRUNNENSTRASSE 105,
13355 BERLIN (GESUNDBRUNNEN)

Reservations highly recommended	berliner-unterwelten.de	U8 (Voltastraße) S1, S2, S25, S26 (Humboldthain)

© HOLGER HAPPEL

THE BEST OF
MODERN CUISINE

Otto's is basically the perfect restaurant, with its modern but warm decor (concrete walls and an open kitchen), lively atmosphere, delicious and inventive cuisine and friendly service ... Places like this are few and far between in Berlin.

Moreover, unlike at most of Berlin's gourmet restaurants, where you have to order a five-, seven- or eight-course menu, at Otto's you can order à la carte, a welcome change.

After working for a number of Michelin-starred restaurants, including Koks (Faroe Islands), Maaemo (Oslo), Loco in Lisbon and Noma's pop-up restaurant in Tulum (Mexico), Berlin native Vadim Otto Ursus, who was born in Prenzlauer Berg (just a stone's throw from the restaurant), returned home to open Otto, which sources all its ingredients from Berlin and the immediate surroundings. Remember to book in advance: the restaurant only seats about 20.

 RESTAURANT OTTO
ODERBERGER STR. 56,
10435 BERLIN (PRENZLAUER BERG)

| THU–MON: 6pm / 11pm | Reservations highly recommended
otto@otto-berlin.net
otto.superbexperience.com | U2 (Eberswalder Straße) |

TRIPPING
IN A PSYCHEDELIC UNDERGROUND STATION

Was the architect on LSD? You'd be forgiven for asking as you watch the psychedelically decorated underground stations on Berlin's U7 line go by, just before Spandau ...

While we're particularly fond of Paulsternstraße (exceptional) and Siemensdamm (also note the spectacular air vents outside), the stations right before, heading west, are also not to be missed: Jungfernheide, Mierendorffplatz, Richard-Wagner-Platz, Wilmersdorfer Straße, Konstanzer Straße and Fehrbelliner Platz.

The last seven stations, from Siemensdamm to Rathaus Spandau, were even listed as protected structures in 2017.

 U7
DIRECTION RATHAUS SPANDAU

Designed by Rainer Rümmler in the early 1980s, these stations are true architectural gems. Appointed chief architect of the Berlin underground in 1964, Rümmler, after fumbling to find an identity for the 50 or so stations he would eventually

build, took inspiration from pop art (which was exploding on the world stage at the time) to design the extension of the U7 line to Spandau. Each station is unique and absolutely worth the trip.

PADDLING IN
'LITTLE VENICE'

In the warm months, Berlin, with its many lakes, rivers and beaches, is a paradise for swimming and boating.

On the western outskirts of the city, but just 20 to 30 minutes by car from the centre, Berlin hides a unique network of small canals that connect branches of various rivers and lakes. The area, south of Spandau and west of Charlottenburg, is fittingly nicknamed 'Klein Venedig' (Little Venice) – all that's missing are the bell towers and Renaissance churches. To explore it, rent a kayak (motorboats are too big) and set off on a fantastic three-hour circuit, including glimpses of this Kolonie's charming little allotment gardens running directly down to the water. Bring along a picnic or get take-away pasta from Il Passetto, the restaurant just across the road from one of the places that rents kayaks.

 **KLEIN-VENEDIG**

Reservations highly recommended

13kanus.de
marina-base.de
der-bootsladen.de

On the other side of town, east of Köpenick, 'Neu Venedig' (New Venice) is equally worth checking out. Treat yourself to a tasty lunch on the water at the Müggelseefischerei or order a picnic lunch from there – the smoked salmon is divine – before enjoying the late afternoon light in a kayak. You can rent one from (among other places) 13Kanus, which is perfectly located and stays open until 8 pm. Two hours is enough to get a good overview of the network of canals that make up Neu Venedig but if you have a bit more time (or a small motorboat), you should definitely consider exploring the wilder surroundings around the Gosener Kanal, south-east of Neu Venedig.

NEU-VENEDIG
MÜGGELSEEFISCHEREI – DORFSTRASSE 13, 12589 BERLIN (KÖPENICK)

KAYAKS
KANUVERLEIH-BERLIN.DE

SAT & SUN (April–Oct.):
10am / 6pm

030 50560758

kanuverleih-Berlin.de

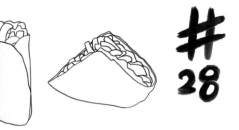

BERLIN'S
BEST KEBABS

Sometimes you don't have the time or the inclination for a long-drawn-out restaurant meal but still want to eat well. The good news is that in Berlin you can.

Among the city's countless doner kebab options, Mustafa's Gemüse Kebab in the west of Kreuzberg is one of the best, hands down.

Crispy bread, vegan options, delicious grilled vegetables … everything is perfect, even the opening hours: until 2am on weekdays and 5am at the weekend.

The only problem with Mustafa's is that it's hardly a secret: the queues can be long (sometimes with waits of more than 30 to 40 minutes!), especially at lunchtime and around 6pm.

Other good places include Rüyam Gemüse Kebab (Gemüse means vegetables in German) and NUR Gemüse Kebap. Beware: some of the well-known and/or historic spots are totally overrated, in our opinion, so don't always rely on the length of the queue.

 **MUSTAFA'S GEMÜSE KEBAB** MEHRINGDAMM 32, 10961 BERLIN (KREUZBERG) €	**RÜYAM GEMÜSE KEBAB** HAUPTSTRASSE 133, 10827 BERLIN (SCHÖNEBERG) €	**NUR GEMÜSE KEBAP** HERMANNSTRASSE 113, 12051 BERLIN (NEUKÖLLN) €
MON–FRI: 10am / 2am SAT & SUN: 11am / 5am U6, U7 (Mehringdamm)	DAILY: 11am / midnight S1, S2, S26 (Julius-Leber-Brücke) U7 (Kleistpark)	DAILY: 10am / 2am U8, S42, S45, S46 (Hermannstraße)

JAZZ LIKE IN
NEW ORLEANS

Yorckschlösschen is a little gem of a jazz club in a gorgeous locale dating back to the 1900s. Even though many Berliners don't know about it, you can always count on spending an excellent evening here in an atmosphere reminiscent of the best New Orleans jazz clubs. ... or perhaps even better as it isn't touristy at all.

Opt for a spot in the main room, facing the musicians.

YORCKSCHLÖSSCHEN
YORCKSTRASSE 15,
10965 BERLIN (KREUZBERG)

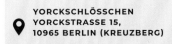

THU–SUN: Music from approx. 8pm / 10:30pm | Reservations highly recommended yorckschloesschen.de | U6, U7 (Mehringdamm)

#30

TRACKING DOWN BERLIN'S **ARCHITECTURAL ODDITIES**

An underground that runs through a house; a giant, 20-metre-high pink tube; a building on top of a bunker; an edifice with a motorway running through it ... Here's a mini-tour of some of Berlin's architectural oddities.

> An architectural UFO

Standing 35 metres high, on the edge of Tiergarten Park, the UT2 building looks like a cross between a giant pink pipeline and a grounded container ship. Even many Berliners don't have a clue what it is. In fact, it's simply an aquatic test facility.

 UT2 BUILDING
MÜLLER-BRESLAU-STRASSE 15,
10623 BERLIN (TIERGARTEN)

Open on Heritage Day or on request:
dms.tu-berlin.de/menue/versuchseinrichtungen/
umlauftank_ut2

S3, S5, S7, S9 (Tiergärten)

> A building over a bunker ▼

Built in 1944–45, the Hochbunker Pallasstrasse couldn't be demolished after the war because the surrounding residential buildings were too close. The solution? They simply built a building on top of it. Spectacular!

 HOCHBUNKER PALLASSTRASSE
PALLASSTRASSE 28,
10781 BERLIN (SCHÖNEBERG)

Not open to the public | U2 (Bülowstraße)

> An edifice with a motorway running through it

Built in 1980, the 600-metre-long 'Schlange' (Snake) has the extraordinary distinction of being one of only two buildings in the world to have a section of motorway running right through it. The insulation is particularly good so that the 3,500 occupants only hear a very slight 'knock-knock-knock' from the traffic in the heart of the building. For an unobstructed view of where the Snake literally engulfs the motorway, head to the southern side of the building. The other construction of this type, the Gate Tower Building, is located in Osaka, Japan.

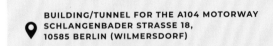

**BUILDING/TUNNEL FOR THE A104 MOTORWAY
SCHLANGENBADER STRASSE 18,
10585 BERLIN (WILMERSDORF)**

U3 (Rüdesheimer-Platz)

> An underground that runs through a house

The old house at Dennewitzstrasse 2 is a real anomaly: it might be the only building in the world that has an underground train running directly through it. This oddity dates back to the 1920s, when the decision was made to run the underground through the building as it was cheaper than destroying it.

**DENNEWITZSTRASSE 2,
10785 BERLIN (KREUZBERG/SCHÖNEBERG)**

U1, U2, U3 (Gleisdreieck)

**We never reveal the 31st address
in the "Soul of" series because it's strictly confidential.
Up to you to find it!**

THE
TIMELESS INN

A meal at this restaurant has to be earned! West of Charlottenburg, just south-west of the lovely Lietzensee lake, you'll see that Google Maps is at a complete loss. So just follow these directions: at the bend in Dernburgstraße, a street (unnamed on Google Maps) leads a little further south. A few seconds later, you'll see a white sign with green letters (also visible from further away on Dernburgstraße), with a gate beneath it that looks locked. It's not. Open it and weave your way along the magical network of dirt pathways that run through these allotments (Kleingärten), typical of Berlin and most of which, like this one, were laid out along railway tracks.

 FOLLOW THE INSTRUCTIONS

FRI & SUN: 1pm / 7pm SAT: 1pm / 9pm	S-Bahn: Messe Nord or U2: Sophie-Charlotte Platz, then a 10–15-minute walk

Now it's up to you: you'll have to walk another five minutes (and through a mini-tunnel) to reach this country inn, far away from what's trendy and on people's lips. Timeless, literally.

The terrace, in its natural surroundings, overlooks the small gardens but also the railway tracks, which gives it a certain charm in the eyes of some while others might be bothered by the frequently passing S-Bahn trains. Contrary to expectations, the food is actually very good.

After lunch, we highly recommend continuing your stroll on the other side of the tracks, where you'll discover a huge network of allotments (reached through another small tunnel, right after the main entrance), which rounds off the one you were in.

MANY THANKS TO

ROMAINE JONGLEZ, for having accompanied me throughout the whole process

LOUIS JONGLEZ, for having followed me by bike to so many unlikely places and for playing ping pong with me in the remotest parts of Berlin

REBECCA GIRARDI, for her invaluable help on every subject, in the choice of places, photos, etc.

FANY PÉCHIODAT, for coming up with the wonderful idea for this collection

SIRAI BUCARELLI, for transcribing Berlin's soul into drawings

KARIM BEN KHALIFA, for the cover

And to all those who helped or accompanied me at one point or another along the way, sometimes without even knowing it: Jürgen Bangmeister, Jacopo Barbarigo, Andrea Bauer, Tinko Czetwertynski, Stéphane Decaux, Uwe Fabich, Mia Ganda, Jacques Garance, Daniel Gerlach, Alexandre Guérin, Dennis Guggenheim, Christina Haufe, Daniel Heer, Katharina Heim, Nicola Henning, Shino Kobayashi, Pauline Loeb, Frédéric Lucas, Raimon Marquardt, Tom & Nadine Michelberger, Vincent Moon, Vadim Otto Ursus Henselder, Luca-Eliza Pretz, Jens Riedel, Steffen Roth, Maxime Rovère, Manuel Roy, Bertrand Saint Guilhem, Mathieu Saura, Géraldine Schwarz, Michael Schöneberger, Tamara Siedentopf, Hemma Thaler, Nicolas Van Beek, Nic Warner, Dylan Watson-Brawn, Kerry Westhead, Carsten Zeiler, Lilith Zinc, Felix, Jan & Gabrielle

This book was created by:

Thomas Jonglez, who also published the *Secret Berlin* guide

Rebecca Girardi, production

Sirai Bucarelli, illustrations

Karim Ben Khalifa, cover photo

Aurélie Saint-Martin, layout design

Emmanuelle Willard Toulemonde, layout

Sophie Schlondorff, translation

Jana Gough, editing

Kimberly Bess, proofreading

Clémence Mathé, publishing

You can write to us at contact@soul-of-cities.com

Follow us on Instagram on @soul_of_guides

THANK YOU

In the same collection:

Soul of Athens
Soul of Barcelona
Soul of Kyoto
Soul of Lisbon
Soul of Los Angeles
Soul of Marrakesh
Soul of New York
Soul of Rome
Soul of Tokyo
Soul of Venice

© JONGLEZ 2022
Registration of copyright: May 2022 – Edition: 01
ISBN: 978-2-36195-394-2
Printed in Slovakia by Polygraf